Listening to God's Whisperings

Listening to God's Whisperings

Ideas to Grasp for Your Enlightened Journey

~Prose and Poetry~

Written and Illustrated by
Lori Wiscombe

Copyright © 2023 by Lori Wiscombe

All rights reserved. No part of this book may be reproduced or transmitted in any form or by any means, electronic or mechanical, including photocopying, recording, or any information storage and retrieval system, without permission in writing from the author. The intent of the author is to only provide information of a general nature for your quest for personal, emotional or spiritual well-being.

ISBN: 978-1-6653-0507-5

This ISBN is the property of BookLogix for the express purpose of sales and distribution of this title. The content of this book is the property of the copyright holder only. BookLogix does not hold any ownership of the content of this book and is not liable in any way for the materials contained within. The views and opinions expressed in this book are the property of the Author/Copyright holder, and do not necessarily reflect those of BookLogix.

⊗This paper meets the requirements of ANSI/NISO Z39.48-1992 (Permanence of Paper)

The author offers sincere thanks and appreciation to Drs. Ronald and Mary Hulnick, Founding Faculty, for their teachings and influence that lead to publication of this book.

The author is most grateful and was inspired in writing the prose, "Rain Forests Capture Earth's Enlightenment" (on pages 85-88), from the book, *The Soul of Money: Reclaiming the Wealth* (publisher: Norton, W.W. & Company, Inc) by Lynne Twist and used terminology with her permission.

011923

*To Ron and Mary Hulnick, my teachers from USM, who gave me
the skills to enlighten my life with room for bliss.*

*To my sons, Kevin Blickfeldt and
Sean Blickfeldt who are my everything in life.*

Contents

Introduction	*xi*

Part One
Hello Enlightenment!

Be open…	3
Second Chances	4
The Power to *Be*	6
Changes Towards Acceptance	9
Counseling In Trio-Alliance	11
ABC's of Living	13
Journey to the 'Bottomed-Out' Ego	14
Growing Pains	15
Spirit's Truth Becomes Tangible	16
My Heart Surrenders—Desire is Enough	18
Creator's Growth	21
Mr. Croak K. (a.k.a. the living frog outside my window) says:	22
Doctor Doolittle Doodling	23
Earth's Tears Resolve Resistance	27

Part Two
Sorrows, Sympathies & Mis-forgivings…

Lessons Are Learned: Finding My Way Back Home	31
Dissipating Beliefs	34
Prayer For Your Own Freedom	36
Like-Minds Collaborate (Mr. B's 'Sky' Entrance)	38
Thy Healing Hand Perceives My Feeling Plan~~Mantra	40
Know your heart's been bleeding…	42
Pot Luck for Stone Soup	43

PART THREE
Rainbows brighten...

I accept me…	47
Make Amends	48
It is my intention…	49
Plea for Miraculous Redefining	50
The Consciousness of Reframing	51
Prayer for Space	53
Wonderous Night of Wonders	54
Being	55

PART FOUR
Joy in its Extent!

Cloud Burst	59
I Am Grounded in My Circle of Joy	60
babbling, bubbly brooks…	61
Mind's Frills Lined with Playing Grounds	62
The Big Garden of Eternal Life	64
Reflective Love	66
Carrying On Exceeds My Limits	67
Would You Believe~~Could You Receive?	69
Dress Rehearsal	71
Conveying My Faith~~Relaying My Soul	73
My How You've Grown!	75
God's Declaration	76
Prayer	77
Q? How does God hear everyone's prayers? Energy Fields	78
Divine Communication	80
Melody from God's Inner Child	81
When You Get Right Down to It…	82
What Is the Measure of A Man?	83
Butterfly Wings	84
Rain Forests Capture Earth's Enlightenment	85

Afterword
Where it all began...

The things we do…to do the things we do	91
Cartoon Comic Strip	92

INTRODUCTION

Have you ever had an inspiring whisper in your ear, or an inspiring idea come to your mind? That is how these prose and poetry were written and designed, waking up to hear encouraging words to live by personally.

In my view, read these prose and poetry, one to two pieces at a time. In this book, *Listening to God's Whisperings,* the second, third and fourth poems, "Second Chances", "The Power to Be" and "Changes Towards Acceptance" mention specific basic skills and terms; grateful teachings provided by University of Santa Monica (USM) Spiritual Psychology program. Its heartfelt influence brings to light, parts of our lives that either makes or breaks our inner peace. This shows how we can choose, respond and change that ebbs and flows in life.

Lighthearted, thoughtful and uplifting prose and poetry commences in Part One with its *Hello Enlightenment!* segment. This is followed by Part Two, *Sorrows, Sympathies & Mis-forgivings* (seemingly unable to forgive yourself or another)… with more profound wholehearted, soul-searching poems depicted during these times. Part Three, *Rainbows brighten…* an empathetic and consoling invitation from God who is soothing our Souls. Part Four, *Joy in its Extent!* brings singing and joy-filled heart-swells making room for bliss with its writings. Also in this section, two poems were written by my father, the late Howard O. Wiscombe. These poems set the mood to help foster others, or as USM would say, I'm "Taking it to the Streets!" Finally, the Afterword section with *Where it all began…* finishes out the book. All-in-all, this book provides and reflects a spiritually enlightened journey upwards, with God encouraging us and cheering for us every step of the way!

PART ONE

Hello Enlightenment!

Be open.

Be patient.

Be believing.

Receive.

"Second Chances"

I feel like we are teenagers again
Getting to know our peeps
Finding ourselves through the eyes of another
"Will I fit in?"... "I'll try this or the other..."
If that doesn't work I'll say, "just kidding!"
And that's OK--
Forgiving.

I feel like we are teenagers again
Getting to know our classmates spiritually
Finding ourselves through the eyes of authenticity
"How I was when you first glanced eyes on me
no longer works for me."
And that's OK--
Compassion lays over me.

I feel like we are teenagers again
"Taking it to the Streets"
Getting to know You as a part of me
Finding ourselves, as we speak
"I will not forget who I AM being me,"
Because that works with genuine simplicity.
As my Self--
LOVE.

"The Power to *Be*"

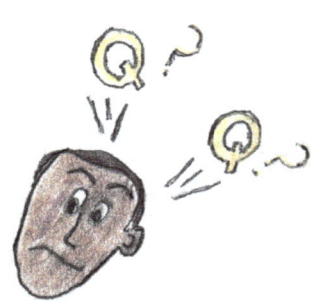

You read
You begin to open up
You ask questions
You set Bedtime Intentions.

You incorporate Basic Skills
Facilitations too
Oh, grant me
Ability to see these through!

I'm here to realign
Resonating Breakthrough
Incorporate Self-Counseling
Seeking wisdom in my refuge.

My intuition, intentions
My imagination invents
The kind of life my talents
Creates exciting events.

I'd like to take Action Steps
Acting "as if"
I have made more room
Completing my incompleteness.

I'm listening to my conscience
I must fulfill my independent will
So, don't spill out every "baby step"
With things I've set out to do.

That's Okay if I soar to greatness
Towards ultimate human freedom
That's Okay with Spirit's forgiveness
Guides me for whom I will become.

While I journey along my path
While I encounter human existence
While I in-store Heartfelt Prizing
While I'm Seeing the Loving Essence.

I'm sinking in the groundwork
Anchored to my Soul
I'm more connected without my ego
Saying, "I told you so."

Mindful, peaceful awareness
Is the place I want to be
I'm granting Self permission
Grateful to choose, respond and change.

My Soul had something missing
I've abandoned old beliefs
My ego now is shrinking
My Heart has room for Bliss.

So, I'm Taking it to the Streets
It may simply be just this:
Using Self experiences
To greater depths in Consciousness.

"Changes Towards Acceptance"

I came upon this train called *Life*
Leaving current destination
Where the world never stops
I'm feeling new changes as reckless.

Will I crash and burn?
Well?…This *f-e-e-l-s* right
Like I felt a time or two before…
Still, it leaves me wanting spiritually *more*.

So, I hopped onto this new train
And the world seems messy
Where no guarantees seem to reside
But, creating along the way.

Turns out it's Love that has all powers!
Headed towards freedom--
Oh! I *can* feel any time I want
I've got all the inner resources.

Perhaps this wild ride, I'll shift and reframe
Perhaps I'm actually *on*
Now riding waves that I can tame
Calls for hope, ease and grace.

Change may be inevitably
Holding Acceptance and Trust
I surrender with dignity
Lessening reluctance and fuss.

Let me ride upon the waves
Let me throw a three-foot toss
Towards actions of new found joy
Revel in my grateful, loving thoughts.

Can it be, I quite like me, all aspects You can see?
Once hidden, I'll integrate with wholeness
Allowing creations, clarity
And compassionate Self-forgiveness.

Turns out there's more to me
I'm guided by gifts of vision
Intuitive aspects tend to appear quite clear
Guess *Spirituality* has its merit.

With this or something better
I'll continue waves of joy
Remembering that my classmates
Certainly have my back.

Gratitude swells deeper straight from my heart
I left my train so long ago
And joined life upon my wave, the rock,
Sure foundation that ebbs and flows

Now I'll hold this space for me…
I'll journey
on…
And *beyond*…

Surf's up!

"COUNSELING IN TRIO-ALLIANCE"

Oh TOLERENCE
Can I count on you
And carry me through
Tomorrow?

ACKNOWLEDGE
My fearful foe
I'll state in bold!
…or perhaps in private.

ACCEPTANCE
What you represent
A leader
And one of God's servants.

INTENTION
Hold the space--
Call for pivotal
Conversation.

TRUST
That triggered pride
Won't stand in way of rights
And decisions.

PRAYER
For softened hearts
While you converse,
Rely and actually listen.

RELEASE
For the highest good
For what the people
Are thinking of…

ISSUES
I'll start with me--
Affect the whole
Of Humanity.

FAITH
Let freedom ring!
Our Call
For less indecisions.

NAMESTE
The God in me
Sees the God in You
Hope and Reason.

"ABC's of Living"

A- adjusting to align, amazingly abundant...
B- *be*, believe, behold! beautifying, be You...
C- creation, charity, can do...
D- divine, demystify, dancing...
E- effortless, expressive, expansive...
F- for and in behalf of God, friendly, familiarity of your Soul and your Soul's desires...
G- grieving the old--opens up for the new, gratitude "great-full"...
H- heart-mind, heartfelt, heart-swells...
I- I AM, inner resources, individualism creates Oneness with Him...
J- joy = jazzed...
K- kindness, kiss, kinsfolk...
L- live, laugh, love, Self-love, loving all Others...
M- marvelous, magnificent, mollify...
N- now, new love, new experiences, new feelings...
O- One, Omnificent...
P- prayer, present, provisions provides...
Q- quiet within, quickened-mind, quirky--but that's just me :) ...
R- remember who You are, rainbows...
S- seeing, sunrays, Soul, Spirituality, Self-forgiveness, Self-worth...
T- tremendous, timely...
U- uniquely You, unstoppable...
V- varied, very creative, very amazing...
W- what a difference You make in the world!...
X- x-traordinary...
Y- You, You are Enough, You the man! You the woman!...
Z- zealous...

~~this or something better...

"Journey to the 'Bottomed-Out' Ego"

I beat my "insistencies"
Of ego-mania chatter
"Protection" shuts down consistently
Kept me "safe" and fatter.

I beat my memories
Of instant, non-stop...feeling sadder
Emotions, "sympathies" depressing me
Clashing, strife-filled clatter.

I like my life remembering
Love filled, heart-swells matter
When I become appreciating
Paths welcome abundant desires.

Life is full of the miraculous
It used to be so sticky
When I maintain my "fabulous"
I see Others with loving essence.

"Growing Pains"

Thank You so much for bringing me here!

I now know who I AM
I'll take it from here, it's my choice to *be*
Though your insistence creates energy pulling me
It's like I want to push back.

Thank You so much for bringing me here!

But I've got it from here
When did I suddenly become not enough
For the spectacular to appear?
I'm whole, let me dwell in my own light of love.

Thank You so much for bringing me here!

I find all my choices within
I believe in my goal: life is interpersonal
While charting my course to begin
Please know this is not personal.

Thank You for saving my life.

"Spirit's Truth Becomes Tangible"

While you are remembering from *before*
Your purpose lies beyond--
While life seems to cycle
Your game face is on.

Your Spirit says, "Awaken"
Your purpose more clear
Questions uprising
Answers inwardly appear.

This sparks *more* to surface
Yet, gifts now align
Each one is a clue for you
Your purpose is divine.

It's not that it's new for you
You have always known--
It's just that your memory
Unlocks in due time.

Life's lessons present itself
Opportunities you'll find
Together you learn from them
Gathers more to refine.

No matter One's curriculum
Call it life's best teachers
All paths journey upwards
Destination's God-aspired.

Until your Earth life captures
All the courses divinely inspired
Until you're more forthcoming
God's mysteries yet unfold.

"My Heart Surrenders--Desire is Enough"

Part of me says it's okay to surrender
Abandoning control
Heading towards the Free--Way!
Another part creeps up
"Slow it down. Let's consider."
Always maintain in what I am saying
Never allowing...only surviving.

It's a matter of trusting
That I will surrender
"Having the faith, doesn't it feel good?"
"Holding the space," I remember
Getting to the place of brotherhood
Knowing I *can* be of assistance
My gift
Loving my place
In the world.

Teaching's my way of bettering the world
Preparing that all I can do is what's right
Owning all parts of me
Makes me feel vulnerable
A truth I won't deny:
"I will not forget who I AM!"
Allowing myself to feel
Allowing myself to get real.

This I give to myself with no fuss
It's how it works, giving myself trust
God is in charge, not me
Aligning myself
Within Earthly Curriculum
Sending love along the way
Dispelling the myth,
"If I'm vulnerable, people will hate me!"
Still, owning all of me
Affords great magnitude.

We are our own magnetic field attracting
Taking dominion over my thoughts
Changing over and over
Until it lines up
If I can't quite believe
Then staying in my desire
It's enough, fruition occurs
Hitting replay and handling it.

If I can't quite surrender, then I will forever
Take good care of myself till I can for another
Holding the space of gratitude in my heart
Knowing my gifts are part of being
Self-worth
Claiming my blessings
Then sending my prayer for relief
Clearing, cleaning and tuning
Refining my intentions
My wisdom comes forth
My energy field thus expanding
While supporting my Soul.

"Creator's Growth"

When life was slow
And life was long
Ideas were slim
And accomplished none.

Now change has come
And life is fast
Quickly dig me
From out of my past.

My mind is rushing
Chaos surrounds
Something inspiring
And deeply profound.

I'm counting on synchronicity
Make it consume me!
Surrounding my angst
Dissolving right through me.

Ultimately doing my best
In creating
Rewarding in life is
That of Being.

"Mr. Croak K.

(a.k.a. the living frog outside my window) says":

"I'm here to remind you
As I'm welcoming your day
I'm here to find you
What stepping stones convey.

Then again at night
As You reach out for the stars!
As You say, 'good night to Today'
The best there is so far.

Sleep till morning's sun rays
Arrive, brighten each and every day
ribbit...
croak..."

"Doctor Doolittle Doodling"

He was really paying attention to the details
Going to bed early...accepting the silly
Doodling the fragile details
Of the early morning sensitive matters
Enjoying the good times
Exceeding the joy
That swells up in his heart
Every day he spent nearly half the time
Walking in his garden
Listening to the birds' divine nature
Satisfied he'd make it good another day
Filling in the details that makes him happy
Existing to create his art
For the people's enjoyment
Loving the way he spends his time
In his mind of garden variety
Of detailed situations in his environment.

The birds exist to bring forth goodness
And wholeness
Holiness divine atmosphere
Peaceful enjoyment resides
In the heart of his goodness
Retired, resigned to do only
That which can be anything good
Reflecting to create the fun
Light hearted notes playing between his ears
Listening to whatever comes from his heart
Carrying wherever his legs will go
Swinging the branches and leaves
Of their homes to say,
"Good morning, dear birdies.
How do you do today?"
"I'm fine, what do you say?"
Minor and major background tweeting
Between neighborhood buddies
Orchestrated symphonies
Of birdie hearts residing
Heart strings striking chords
Of melody meadow larks.

What's the possibility of living
In this simple existence?
Sufficiency mimics
The Big Garden of Life
Realizing the separate and wholeness
Of your Being
Its peacefulness as your teacher
Of creative parts
To your Soul
Happiness exists within
For whatever confronts your way
With outer events
That play out in any given way
Drawing from its lessons
Recorded wisdom
An offering to children of God
The openness you feel
Creates expansions of the heart in people
On planet Earth.

How else does World Peace occur?
It, transforming the light of a few
Then carries out greater service
To even more
Bringing about joy
Straight from the bottom of your hearts
Touching the lives of others
With that same emotion
Splashes of color
Dancing with musical-artistic variety!
Inspiring others
To create their own best niche
Turns to ingenious talents
Growing until they too bloom
A recognition of their own inspired thoughts
Transforms new beliefs
Cranks out heartfelt intentions
With such grace and ease
This inspired goodness is beautiful to Thee.

"Earth's Tears Resolve Resistance"

Sunrise between the treetops
Clouds' existence puffs away
"Deafening" silence takes lofty precedence
Ensuring nature's say.

Morning announcements soon commence
Birdies' tweeting accompaniment
Daybreak-doves' cooing is through
Squirrels' route pursuing.

Now, man enters the animal kingdom
Creatures pose with keen awareness
New visitors stepped in by "freedom's rights"
Their presence, evidence of extinction.

Lessons learned from time to time
Perhaps, serious in nature
Oh, how man *now* worries so
Of Earth's delicate condition.

Can it be that man made things
Are made more thoughtfully?
Can it be that nature brings
Presenting a new rendition?

History does repeat itself
But is man now apt to listen?
Look at New Earth's purpose, please
Creation's moments, anomalies.

New wonders exist miraculously
Just collaborate with utmost precision
You see? Nature's answer stands by patiently
Guided by Gods' magicians.

PART TWO

Sorrows, Sympathies & Mis-forgivings...

"Lessons Are Learned: Finding My Way Back Home"

My daily morning walk in California
Started same as always, same as before
Its usual brisk chill in the air beats about my cheeks
Then, just like that...it's lifeless, seizes
Freezes my usual thoughts of morning awe
Is it me or is this twilight becoming just too eerie?
I cannot seem to wrap my mind
Around what's sudden and dreary
Within only seconds notice
"Shhhh! What was that?"
Malibu's beauty...it _DOES_ seize to amaze me!
As I am startled
And shaken…

Silence is all I heard
Then deafening
I wait--
"There!"…I point long distance
Distinctive, senseless
Chattering of birds once tweeting
And singing to my heart
Creates insistent holler--
Crows above my head
Their circling heckling hackles
Mock me: "You surely do not matter!"
Now I seem to listen for anything close to reason
These gorgeous surroundings come back to me closer…
Too close for comfort…taunts me
Clear this make-shift atmosphere
As Alfred Hitchcock's perfect muse
Playing Mother Nature's orchestra
Sings off key with less sane "clatter"...

THE BIRDS!

"No, it just can't be!"
I ran back for the life of me--
My mind seems to be crashing
Like rhythmic waves speed up against me
Inside my own "cliff side manor"
It's gathering, building…hisses
Slams as if it's "microphoned" splatter

Gone! My love of nearby beauty
Stirs within my Soul
Like a thief at night in Malibu
I calm insistent voices--
That shout, "Get Out!"
"Your life is now in danger!
You have everything to lose
Your belongings will be scattered
Your sense of being devalued."

"Okay! I am on it!"
Mr. B., my cat and I
Know all that seems to matter
Are my lessons learned--
Yet, I gather my belongings to satisfy this urge
I arrive into safety, but not without its drama
My car breaks down while traveling
Though I'm safer among the kindness of world strangers
Then who I once relied on

My sense of well-being is now restored
Pink bubbles show reflections
Of this crash course curriculum
So difficult yet,
Definitely well spent
Miracles are loading
Gratitude and swelling of my heart,
"Hello St. George!
You're looking spectacular!"
With wiggle room to spare
I continue to marvel
Setting sights on Red Rock's welcoming
Its beauty and fan-fare…

Hurrah!
I learned--
The kind of life to *Be*
If I hadn't lived out "Malibu"
I'd never win this right:
Live out what I am born to do
And give it all my might!
"Don't give away your life
To another's moments,
Grief or strife!"

"Dissipating Beliefs"

Do I have everything to lose
Or, do I have everything to gain?
Is my present Self any different
Or has it stayed the same?

When my surroundings, plans and dreams
Take a slandered turn side-way
Such as Hitchcock's warped, starved beauty
Tends to sport musing for THE BIRDS...

When lies and deceit
Present nothing but actual fraud
When heartfelt, hopeful avenues
Unravel at its seams.

When God's favorite creative beauty begins to go awry
Like I need to un-ring the bell I've rung
That tarnished into rust
My lesson now to swallow is, it's ok to get it wrong.

And maybe this residual chaos
What Gurus say appears
Right before the brass ring I grasp
And before I clip my wings.

I'll pick up precious pieces
What's left here seems so scarce
However, holding on allows some reminisce
I'll continue to carry on and watch it materialize--

Okay, I'll watch...
I'll remain...
I'll manifest...
I'll change!

"Prayer For Your Own Freedom"

London bridges falling down

Know your bleeding heart has found

Truth, enlightenment now sees the way

In every aspect within you say,

"I need Thee every hour."

Lost time strands you beneath Big Ben's tower

Amidst swaying treetops

Bends you closer

Binds your story of the price to pay

Leans towards you.

Fraying fringes around your heart

Suggests your "matters"

Are where you'll start

To thine own Self wilt thou be true?

Is much more fortunate for you.

You're known
As "Great Britainy"
Tried to keep
With utmost scrutiny
Pains deep.

But you build back bridges reaching towards your heart
No more secrets that keep you apart
Trust your own divine essence and Soul's desires
Large answers are beneath you
Only makes for liars.

Truthful-Love of which you admire
Sets you free from what chains your Soul
"Breathe deep" mends bridges over troubled waters
Fall back on making right by you
Your path transpires.

"Like-Minds Collaborate (Mr. B.'s 'Sky' Entrance)"

I see a glorious habitat
Of animal creatures looming about
My cat, Mr. B. enters gingerly
I whisper, "This is where it's at!"

Be nice to Mr. Chimpanzee
He'll point about quite accurately
He says, "Climb up Banana Tree
And pick a meal for me times three."

Mr. B. agrees and afterwards, climbs down
He sits next to Chimpanzee,
"Scratch my head continuously
I'm now content to sleep (meow...yawn)."

Be kind to Proud Tiger, please
"I'm One in your ancestry.
Let's hide behind tall blades of grass
And watch shadows-dancing mysteries."

"Let's run wild, fervently
Long strides tend to get us there.
Together we will finally
Begin to play what's fair."

Please share among fun monkeys' glee
Their make-shift play ground's welcoming
Try to "friend" the tall giraffes
Walking in rhythm is a knack.

Mr. B., I hope I can convey
His plan for you, won't you embrace?
Enjoy the life you've waited for
I'm sure you remember from before--

The kind of peace you gave to me;
Empowered service on Earthly Life.
You'll find the place worth looking for
Oh, how I long to reunite.

So... fascinating creatures teach:
Their mindful, peaceful stirring about
Helps humans realize life's extent
Creation's love reunites beyond--

"Thy Healing Hand Perceives My Feeling Plan~~Mantra"

Thank You for shedding light
Overseeing my brain
While every nook n' cranny seeks
Receptive cells ingrained.

Each wrinkle lends unfolding
Deep inside my head
Heals DNA-soul seared cells
Scorched by stroke at birth.

Thank You for spreading Light's presence
While overseeing my senses
Compile mild mangled systems
Into wild strengthened synapses.

While desiring to hear Others' Qualities
Reminds to see their Loving Essence
I'd much rather speak of Thee
Then complain of script-filled nuisance.

Thank You for shining down on me
I'll use my voice more softened
Speaking from my Heart-Mind, I'll ask that
He connects these both with blessings.

Shining sacred sun rays
Nourishes my conscious-minded conscience
Speaking in terms that compliment
Fills my gut-filled bodily system.

Thank You again for *thinking* of me
With Christ-like, love-filled Qualities
When I ask for Thy hand in these
It goes *beyond* Man's reasons.

Thank You so much for *giving* to me
God-sent Aspects throughout my body
Mind-body-soul blessed with clarity
While journeying throughout its seasons.

I'm Breathing...

Know your heart's been bleeding.

Suffering becomes insufferable.

Throw your Self in serving.

God's will announces recovery.

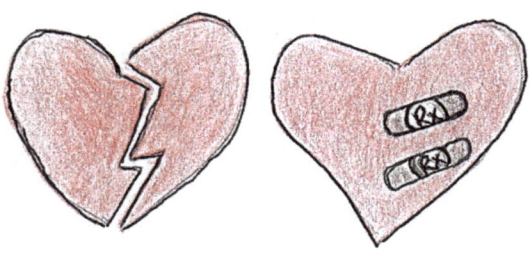

"Pot Luck for Stone Soup"

Start with a big one
The one so disdained
And currently self-contained
Place the stone in a pot preset to boil
Add a mixture
A garden variety
All ready to toss out.

Temperature is rising
Are you still "stirring the pot?"
Then it is still brewing--
Wait! There she blows!
Stone is well done
Timed for giving it away
Don't pick it back up before you walk away.

Just an appetizer before serving Self-forgiveness
Okay…I forgive my Self for judging myself
And other things
Convey
Release
Fill with Love
Measure for Success.

PART THREE

Rainbows brighten...

I accept me
All of me
I accept me implicitly
I Love God subsequently.

"Make Amends"

Spend time believing
My word resides within
Mend ties receiving
A closer relationship.

Find time residing
Your inner thoughts begin
Remind your Self confiding
While peace restores again.

It is my intention

To bring to your attention:

All things are possible

When life begins with God.

"Plea for Miraculous Redefining"

Oh! My Savior Jesus Christ
I am ready to surrender the useless in my life
Won't you clear my mis-forgivings in my tired war-torn Soul?
Help bring to mind with clarity, resistance I controlled.

I say I want to relinquish self-blaming known to me
My tendency to push deep down to places dark and bleak
Though, I seem to delay what's possible
Reminding me I'm wondrous by embracing such beliefs.

But then, again my doubts creep up
From somewhere else inside
I call on Thee to heal and love
Send light to what's confined.

I gather free-form writings under pressure, *written* strife
It's burning fuel now purges deep inside my living Soul
I gather ashes' residue, releasing all what hides
I'm farther on my avenue, now open, life's repose.

So, thank You my Redeemer
Having died for all of Us
I lay to rest what's possible--
Healing is creating Self accomplishments.

"The Consciousness of Reframing"

Have you ever wished and dreamed?
Stepped into the "accomplished"
Thoughts of living well and just like that no longer seems
The life you lead outlived its purpose felt.

Changes and signs come in many forms
So, life starts looking a little warped
Since resistance prevents you looking head on
Messages sent seem so inept.

And God's presence intervenes
Although blessings tend to be disguised
Until later safety, clarity and time reveals
You're grateful for life's pivotal surprises!

Creative gifts perceive you well
Look within to guide you
Inspiration presents well-meaning heart-swells
Listening to find what serves you.

And then your travels spare the gem you've sought
Tagged as your new found friend worthy of you
You finally see the plaguing "hows???"
Reveal answers fervently.

"Will I continue this path, I presented to me?"
Well...I actually discovered it after I could see
My past is really quite honorable
I can draw on lessons innumerable.

The trick is—I swapped out old regrets
A paradigm shift allows the miracle
I'll never change anything what lead up to Now
"Impossible" spells—I'M POSSIBLE!

I have a gift I'd like to tell
Of your accomplishments
And what can heal
Become your guiding forces

To find You~~

"Prayer For Space"

Please clear all mis-beliefs
With apologetic humility
"Let go and believe in me."
It's better that way within humanity
I'm paddling through new territory
Apparently, I've got talent
I slapped with Self-doubts…

I cleared harsh things I said to me
Now space is made for me to be me
Yet I maintained disbelief
How hard it is to really see?
I cared what others thought of me
I am great in the eyes of God
I'll Accept now my place with Thee
Here on Earth to feel Peace.

"Wonderous Night of Wonders"

Have you ever done something
"Just for me"
To not work out
Not supposed to be?

I believe
It was about
Trying to become
What you have dreamed.

But then again
There's more to see
Because Thou risked
It in the name of me.

You believe
Becoming great
Takes some risks
In becoming right.

Look at wonders
Beyond measure!
Behold what covers
Night of creatures!

"Being"

Know your past is honorable
While lessons learned innumerable
Affords one to be profitable
When my word instills good faith.

My way becomes arrangeable
While human beings confiding
My word affords the capable
Heart's inner source residing.

Peace
Good Will
Restores
Earth.

PART FOUR

Joy in its extent!

"Cloud Burst"

Oh, Father in Heaven
Please humble me more
To think of Thee
Like from before--

Why don't I see
The kind of Life
Paved for me
Growing wise?

When all it takes
I tend to smile
"Happy" makes
The dose to swallow.

I'd like the chance
My choice to be
When it rains, let's dance
Let the storm rise freely.

And when the dust dissolves
Along with strife…
Arrive, assess
Arise and shine.

"I Am Grounded in My Circle of Joy"

Dreaming was never as good as it is now!
Processing, creating invites great power
Igniting the spectacular
Adding much desire…

While worries creep in on your future
Stop with what festers
While holding such thoughts fleeting
Why not create You as the winner!

babbling, bubbly brooks
rushing, winding, trickling
makes me want to jump a jot
for its cool, kooky feeling.

"Mind's Frills Lined with Playing Grounds"

Pink bubbles, pillows puffy
Fairy-Angels, unicorns fancy
These are Universe's Candy Lands
Looking through glasses of magical lens:

Traveling inside swaying willows
Leafy dollops of fringed uniform
All of which I aspire to dwell
Due to Debara's merry-filled story tales.

Free-spirited, playful giggling
Causes well-meaning heart-swells
Atmospheric nature gingerly riveting
Airborne excitement, heartfelt.

Out from beyond lies no cloudy clouds
Nor grey smoke lurking beneath the ground
Striking upside-down phony frowns
Nay, woes of gloomed-filled life of strife.

All my life I want to *Be*
I conquer mighty ego pleas
All my wishes while standing tall
Are fun-filled visits-lined wishing wells.

Heart shaped harps
With angels sings
Bow ties atop
Birds' illuminating wings.

Seeing is Believing
But setting free One's own mis-beliefs
Send inner frets fleeting while
Master-filled Miracles keeps on redeeming.

Co-creating wonders are much like these!
Magical expressions ignite synchronicities
Creating life's destiny while playing musical dances
Inspiring One's life, becoming quite precious.

"The Big Garden of Eternal Life"

Oh! Father in Heaven,
Is it fair to be homesick from Thee,
Even though my memories
Shielded from pre-mortality?

I think even my cat misses
The Big Garden of Life
Where anxious "mommy-owners" do not exist
Where perfectness of nature allows mingle and mix.

Where creatures looming day and night
Eyeing others to simply pass by
Where all of it is Home, but our choices define our living.
Diverse matters of the heart are One's created blessings.

I see panoramic scenery of Tree-Boundaries
Divine creations known to man-kind
Love-finding miracles spring forward, blossoming
And time-filled centuries erased by Father Time.

Dreamy, lazy "liaisons" welcoming to say,
"Good morning,
I find you beautiful
More and more in every way".

Hazy, misty atmosphere gloats
Sweet shimmering to convey,
"I exist simply
Because you wanted it this way."

All-in-all, I am centering to align
With love-like living
Call it Rumi's Field
Or Anita's heartfelt dreaming...

It's when we are sitting nearby God
And capture Soul's envisioning
The Big Garden is engulfed from sea to shining sea
Reeling, its color country, discovering civilization once more.

The Big Garden happening
Has past and future seams unraveling
New Creations live in Present form
Just as other worlds before...

"Reflective Love"

Today, I marvel at the ocean waves
Oh, how it signifies the beauty, calms my qualms
Conveys the extent how it smacks against cliffs
In rhythmic sounds and timely Oms.

With Today's timing I seek my God
Admits waiting for me to seek
While I rely on His kindness and love
How He protects, how I feel complete.

When I generate, replenish my love
My "battery" soars from up above
When I can go back to what I commit
I know that love is what He is made of.

However I say what I convey
God knows I am imperfect
Yet working with How I say
Please know these are things I've reflected.

"Carrying On Exceeds My Limits"

Yesterday, I had an extraordinary day
Substitute teaching mostly twelve year old boys
This time of year I usually brace myself for worse
With only ten days left of school.

But, this day when kids were all through
Putting away assignments-now done-nothing left to do
I stood up and gazed out to all worthy Souls
My arms outstretched, I gave **three--rhythmic--claps**.

Another realized his own beat then, added a rap:
"We will, we will--rock you" boom boom
"We will, we will--rock you" boom boom
All involved in their own rhythmic way.

I broke out in a smile, this moment stood still
And then with my presence was all that I needed
I heard each give their wish as adults,
In the real world, contributing, their own "carrying on."

I dreamed later that night...
I stood and waited in line
An Award Night, so real receiving, "job is well done"
I'm amazed with no doubts of this other world sphere.

Awakened-- I looked out the window
Broke into gaze--
I saw that my poems that God really authored
His hand in all things, opportunities offered.

I stood on a hill, I looked out to see
My real world in motion, ignited with force
I see all along while journeying my path
I thought I'd "arrived", but I am actually "carrying on."

"What's that?", you say... *my "carrying on?"*
I'm glad you would ask
I'm learning... residing within
Then, move right along.

"Carrying on" is His conscious lesson
"Taking it to the Streets", another way to mention
Curriculum's lined up, school always in session
I stand rather tall, after all's not forgotten.

Let me just say in my own little way
Thank You so much while residing within
My gratitude towards heaven--
My life, "carrying on" ...and that's simply Okay--

"Would You Believe~~Could You Receive?"

Why did I think this could be causally meant?
I ask for your hand in it all
You've heard this argument since life is well spent
Heard this all against you in the name of "logical."

Dear God, what would you like to say?
Could it bother you a little bit so?
Finally comes what you'd like to convey
Non-belief is commonly known.

In terms of drawing nearer to God again
What I would like to say?
What about coming to terms, drawing nearer to God
What I would like to say?

Could it be that one may fall to crisis-mode?
Would it be that one says, "I've failed…"
How can one recoup once more?
"How?" …after so dismayed?

When I think of utter disbelief
Going back down this past-life path
How about it's turned around
Test it out with faith to see what is found.

It could make more sense
Life's open to receive
You realize your faith's
Now the size of a mustard seed.

Just try it as if it's an experiment
Hypothesis...acting "as if"
Putting it to the test...
Putting a little bit to the test...

Figure it out with a little help
Go ahead, you're no longer alone
Asking of God for a little help
It's the last thing left; you see you've revived.

It's more work to push beliefs down deep inside
Then to open a little, bit by bit
Just let it within actually try to come out
Pour it out and see what's about.

Could it be that God
Is what you believe?
What love is made of?
What would it be about?

I'm asking you, gather your existence--all of you
Practicing, you value His presence
I'm sending Christ-like love from me to you
You mean more to me than ever realized before!

"Dress Rehearsal"

I think today was a dress rehearsal for Christ to come
Oh! ...how the clouds shown with majesty
Illuminating...puffy on puffy
Sprouting sun rays beckoning
"Look up here! Look!"

Grand gestures of rays leading.
I listened, passed people in searching--
Deep in the steel blue sky
Highest of high sunbeams contending
As no one dares reason, why?

Forging on, the morning, just radiating!
Nature gives up its day breaking sound waves
For a new note takes charge
The trumpets now lending
Non-stop, "Hark!" angels are raving.

The New World appears
And the creatures take notice
Scurrying squirrels and rabbits in fury
Then, stop...
Look towards with what seems to matter.

Silence is golden
Except "violins" slight stirring.
At last! Christ takes stage center
Propped solely on clouds' pulpit
He--is--risen!

Mercy performs
With this I envision
We stand a little taller
His children are chosen
Making claps knowing One cannot falter.

The curtain stays open
Its backdrop of beauty
Christ once was risen--
Now masters His grace
Acknowledges our peace.

This seems more precious
His greatest performance
We take upon Him
His star-beaming glory and this way of Being
Happens to be life's treasured gem.

"Conveying My Faith~~Relaying My Soul"

Oh, Father in Heaven!
So much to convey
There's so much inside of us each
Please know I've held, so let me relay
There's more I've felt
There's more I've to say.

Oh, Father
I've needed to say
How gratitude has me engulfed
I stand all amazed
I share all for Thee
I'd rather I stood near you so.

It's likely I'll grow old here on Earth
It's finally occurred to me, oh!
The way that I think of myself isn't the same
It's possibly something I know
Please help me believe
Help me realize Self-worth.

Oh, Father
What you can see
Can it be true?
Just how my existence and growth
Can actually be what you hope in me?
How do I simply release?

Oh, Father in Heaven!
It's actually me
I know that you visually see
Can it possibly be that I take after Thee?
Would you guide my path set for me?
Will you see that I help others, finally?

"My How You've Grown!"

"Could it be that you are greater, than
Words can ever convey?
So much so, it's more than
Other worlds displayed.

Could it be your memory
Unlocks its fraying gates?
Spend time listening
I've important things to say.

I speak and you submit
It's something I believe.
My words comfort you
Especially your hour of need.

My time incorporates
Acceptance now has formed
Spend time receiving me
All blessings are in store."

"God's Declaration"

Let's take care of something please
I am finding it just can't wait
Try to believe I have prepared a way
Know this: My way is my word.

Let's divide time more honorably
On the way towards upward trails
How it winds up happening
Is actually yours to tell.

I will see you all the way through
Formidable change is pivotal
Try to feel with your Heart-mind too
With God, all things are possible.

Prayer

How they're written on my heart
How they're imprinted on my heart
It's only a matter that you start.

Prayer
It's the soul's sincere desire
My Father in Heaven
And my Savior I admire.

Prayer
My soul acquires
My words convey
Seeks acceptance of my heart to say:

Prayer is the Soul's sincere desire.

Q? How does God hear everyone's prayers?

"ENERGY FIELDS"

Mine is an acclimation of sorts
That has prior repetitive action
Yours is a learning curve
Filled with new ignited passion.

Energy stems from matter
And mine is resurrected
Yours gets closer and closer
To becoming quite perfected.

Acclimation seems to hold the key
To life's resistance
Spend time visiting me
And I will lift You in your mission.

Searching something deep inside
Gathers, becomes aware
Choreographed Quantum Leaps
Design your new found travels...

tho'...

Searching is nearer and dearer
Closer than you think
If you want to understand *beyond*
Then remain true to your own provisions.

Mysteries then unfold because
You have learned to listen
Asking is truly of your beliefs
Takes you past Man's reasons.

Conquer life's battles and woes
Which sets you free and composed
You're rediscovering just what your gifts
Have always been in the upcoming enlightened season.

"Divine Communication"

How do you think Father in Heaven conveys
To each one of his children?
Through energy fields that acclimate
And refined intuition.

Staying close and centering oneself
Through guided meditation
Sends rising frequency in bodily cells
To perfect communication.

Spending time and energy this way
Brings to one a great desire
Finding sublime peace and joy
And ask anything God-aspired.

Finding ways to improve Oneself
Results along Journey's growth
Believing prayers will acclaim a life
To ponder, gaze and suppose.

Guided choreographed steps fulfill
Heart-minded synchronicity
Remembering you are fully capable
Becoming one of His chosen reuniting.

It's all designed as abundant simplicity
Realizing who you will become
It's finding Spirit's source while reminiscing
On how God and You are One.

"Melody from God's Inner Child"

Spend a little time with me
I am always comforting
Find a little smile to wear
Then one can never 'er go wrong.

Suddenly you begin to know
This can all be for your growth
Finally, you look to find
The energy to feel sublime.

I am always found to say
Much can really go your way
Frowning never was for me
Wondering how this could ever be?

Stay right here close by my side
And you may want to confide
Friends can show that they can be
Proof that you are Love to me. <3

"When You Get Right Down to It..."

I feel something miraculously coming on
In the way my existence carries on
Spend time believing in Me
And I will see to it, the rest is on me.

Find time receiving my way
I tend to desire, hope and convey
Mend lives discovered your way
Remind; I'm headed your way.

Believe, utter important words
Conceive your imagined thoughts and concerns
Rely on Me with much extent
Contrive not, from tensions sent.

For Me, I've relayed my word
From Thee, my energy soars
Finally, purpose speaks to my heart
Uniting my Soul that sets me apart.

Complete while residing within
For me, I'll abide by Him
Factoring on my abilities
Captures Souls' lives mattering.

"What Is the Measure of A Man?"

What is the measure of a man
As viewed in the passing scene?
What is good or acceptable
Or what is perceived as mean?
Who sets the standard for our behavior
That's measured in reputation?
Who keeps score, and why?
Since that determines our station.
If it is goodness that's admired
And considered essential
Then why do
"Good guys never win."
If love of money is the root of all evil
Then tell me if you can,
Why the world pushes and shoves
To get next to that wealthy man?
I measure Me. As no one else can.
The key of course is **integrity**.
The certainty a man has of himself.
It is living true to how I see me.

Howard O. Wiscombe

"Butterfly Wings"

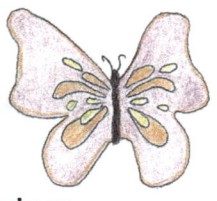

Man was not made as butterfly wings
Or Bright feathered birds at birth,
Not like exquisite flowers or granite peaks,
We were simply created of earth.

But one thing we were given
No other creature has,
Was intelligence and freedom of choice
To follow His plan and reward
Promised by the Master's voice.

We were not as is nature, dressed
In the same penguin tuxedo
Or programmed to sing only one song.
We were taught what was right,
Or if we chose, to do what we knew was wrong.

What a privilege it is when you reflect
We can choose our own cocoon,
To be found forever within this body,
Or burst out - - to be a God with Him.

In a world filled with dollars and eminent scholars
Do we really know why we are here?
It's to overcome weakness and early faults;
To lend a hand and a word of cheer.

Howard O. Wiscombe

"Rain Forests Capture Earth's Enlightenment"

Bleeding hearts and voices
Holler through the sky
To save camping grounds of homes
And their Souls' lives
Success or failure happening to One
Occurs in Others
The Rain Forests are Open for ALL to
Breathe
Clearing the sky, an outpouring of love
Shatters selfish dreams
Perpetuating *more is better*
And *there's never enough*
Sprouting sun rays
Promise
Divine living for all.

When Teachers, the Leaders
Angels, the Heroes
Chiefs all align
For the Commonality in Good
Sufficiency leads us and guides
Proving Heart as the conduit
Speaks to early childhood dreams in
Each individual on Earth
Each host in Heaven
Finding your way
When you choose for yourself
The only person you save is You
The path lies within that Leads us the way
For your voice
Speaks for Others.

Happiness is not a product
To consume and gobble
Peace is not a commodity to trade--
It provides
Sales do not exist among God's trials,
It's tribulations and subsequent lessons
Learn from your past
But stand in direction
Present to You
Seeing money
In the way to confirm its avenue
Towards Greater Good
Your Calling lies within
If You truly Intend.

Trusting You to
See your way through
Compassion
Shedding Light
A new founded law
Having enough room
Through the doors of your heart
An integral moment
Lies pivotal to your needs
Feel Called and your moment
Directs
Sufficient resources shines light
Hear what they say but look to your heart
Leading the way.

Interested persons have their own solutions
Inner resources residing within
Shaking hands of agreement
Rolling up sleeves in organized achievement
Happens when Eagle and Condor
Fly in existence
Cheers from on high
Stir Heart-minds together
Till the Earth's answers
Brings Self-sufficiency, true pride, inspiring beliefs
Calling you to Partner
With those who Collaborate.

Bring the Heroes, the Angels
Bring the Teachers and Leaders
Inspired Chiefs by design
Putting their heads together
In helping a nation
Raising up each generation
Of faithful providers
Now the story begins to
Speak
Having spoken the Truth
Dispelling the greed
Smearing myths of falsified fear.

It, spreading wildly, devastating
The Forests
Destroying all life
"O-n-l-y YOU can prevent…"
Know this!
You're Called to answer needful events
Education is Lovely--
Though Love
Brings Availability
This kind of solution invites:
Self-reliance
Peace
In Your Heart
Prosperity Among Souls.

AFTERWORD

Where it all began...

"The things we do . . .
...to do the things we do"

I wake up nightly
In the middle of the night
I lay back promptly
My bed pulls me in.

Sleep! I want more sleep!
But my cat, Mr. B. knows better
He gets up, plops on the floor
And **stares** at me, waits as my predictor.

How does he know?
Poems will start writing in my head
I fight the impulse to take my "foe"
"Stay in bed, instead."

This dance we do seems ritual
Formulating in my mind
Then, I'm thankful time's well spent!
Wow! Inspiration *arrives* quite punctual.

Let the poems begin...

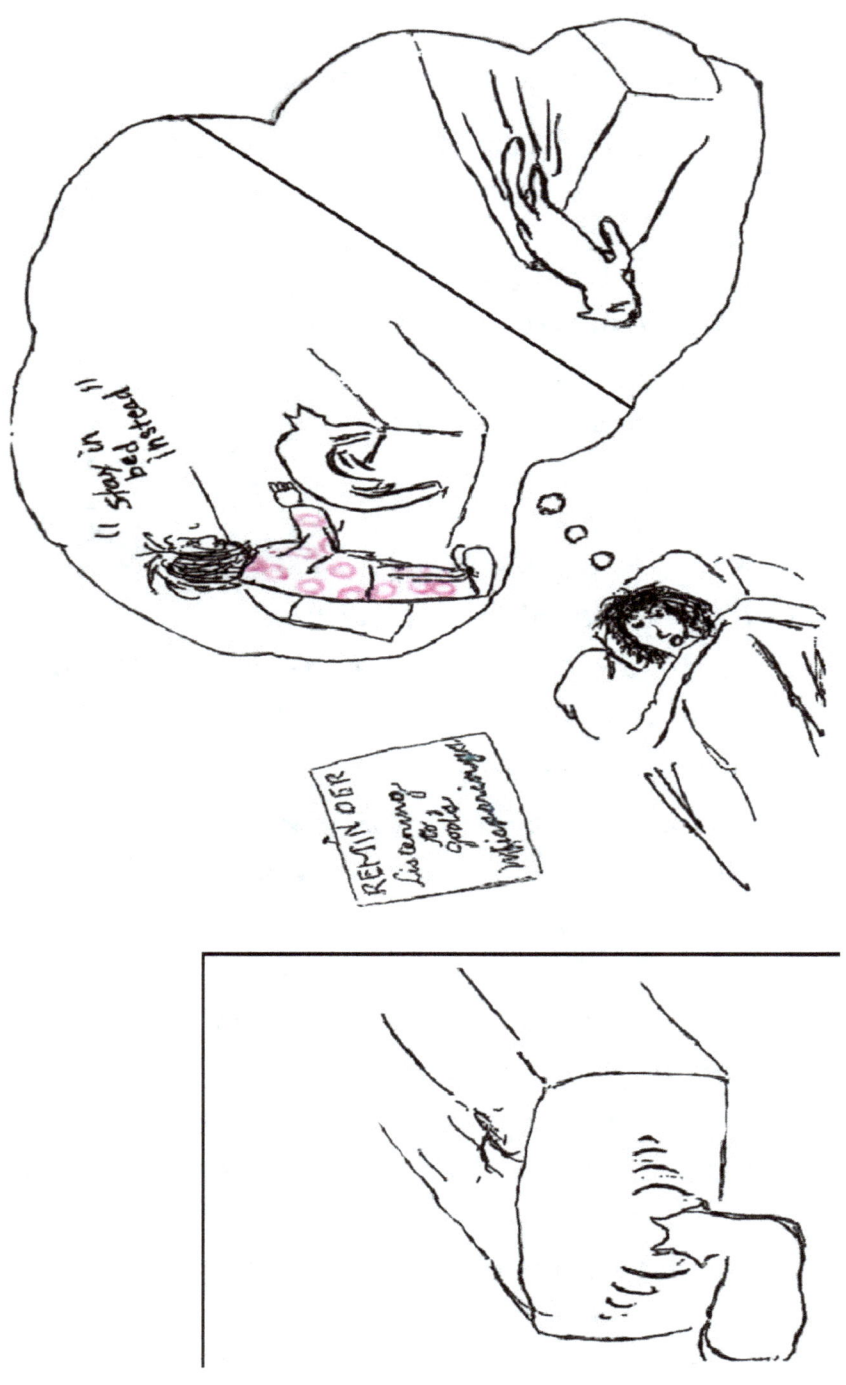

About the Author

Lori Wiscombe was born in Salt Lake City, Utah and lived in Bountiful, Utah until 2009; having two sons and one granddaughter. She received her Bachelors of Science in Psychology from University of Utah in 1992, and then a Special Education teaching certificate from Utah State University Extension in 1996.

Ms. Wiscombe enjoyed many years employed as a substitute teacher and continued doing so while attending University of Santa Monica, enrolled in the Spiritual Psychology school program from 2011-2012. Its influence there helps facilitate promptings of spiritual prose and poetry for her. She now resides in St. George, Utah.

www.ingramcontent.com/pod-product-compliance
Lightning Source LLC
Chambersburg PA
CBHW052207090526
44583CB00017BA/2414